My Letter to Daddy

Written and Illustrated by Renee Walker

My Letter to Daddy
Copyright © 2018 by Renee Walker
My Pride Books
Sherwood, Arkansas

Manufactured in the U.S.A.

All rights reserved.
No part of this book may be reproduced or transmitted in any manner without prior written permission from the publisher.
This book may be purchased in bulk for promotional, educational, or business use.
Hardcover also available. Please contact sales@mypridebooks.com

ISBN: 978-0-692-12750-6 (Paperback Edition)
ISBN: 978-0-692-10526-9 (Hardcover Edition)

Library of Congress Control Number: 2018904557
Summary: Military children write to their dad while he is away, recalling memories, and expressing support and love.

Acknowledgments:
Editors: Alice Zimmerman, Jane Greenwald, Verna Dean Greenwald, and Janet Greenwald
Special thanks to: Samantha Wells and Meagan Counts
Photo credit: Kaylie Walker

This book is dedicated to:
My two sweet kids,
and all the military members
and their families who make sacrifices every day.

Hi Daddy, it's me!
How are you? I am fine.
You've been gone awhile.
I really miss you.
I think about you all the time.

Before you left,
I got extra hugs and kisses
when saying goodnight.
You told me to keep my chin up
and that everything
would be alright.

Saying goodbye was really hard. Watching you walk away made me sad. You're a very special guy to me. After all, you are my Dad.

You told me you were leaving,
but I didn't understand
until you were gone.
I stood there waiting
for you to come back to me,
but life continued on.

I miss greeting you at the door
as your car rumbled
into the garage.
I would help you
untie your combat boots
as you took off your camouflage.

I think about our time together
filled with games
and endless giggles.
I enjoyed our hugs and kisses
that turned into horseplay
and tons of tickles.

Daddy, Daddy, I love you. I love you, and I know that you love me.
My heart is strong, I'm holding on, however far you may be.

I can only imagine
the new places you are going
and the exciting things you'll see.
Make sure you keep
an eye out for treasures
so you can bring some home to me.

Daddy, Daddy, I love you.
I love you,
and I know that you love me.
My heart is strong,
I'm holding on,
however far you may be.

Tonight, I'll blow you a kiss,
so get ready to catch it in your hand.
I want you to know it's a special
"I love you" message that I planned.

I'll jump into your arms to hug the one I've been waiting so long to see. Even after all the time you've been gone, I'll be so grateful when you're finally back home with me!

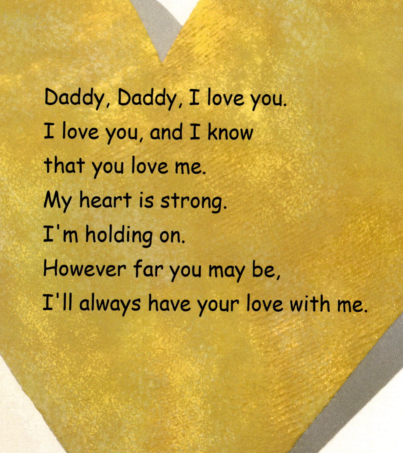

Daddy, Daddy, I love you.
I love you, and I know
that you love me.
My heart is strong.
I'm holding on.
However far you may be,
I'll always have your love with me.

Author's Note:

Deployments are difficult. They are filled with many emotions and challenges. In addition to dealing with my own feelings, my two children were struggling to understand why their father was gone for months on end. Their limited language skills sometimes led to frustration and misbehavior. This inspired me to write a book using simplified, childlike language to help my children express their various emotions, understand the purpose of military separation, and be reminded that they are loved.

Use these questions to help guide children to open up about problems they may face and yet find silver linings where happiness can still be found despite their struggles.

What makes you feel sad?

What makes you happy? (toys, sports, reading?)

Where can you find love or friendship? (family, friend, pet, religion?)

What are you grateful for? What do you appreciate in life? (health, friends, food?)

What can you do to make your parents proud of you? (clean your room, help in the kitchen, help a neighbor?)

Made in the USA
Columbia, SC
16 July 2020